Daily O₁ Language (DOL)

Copyright © 2022 Anam Cara Cat

PLEASE VISIT MY WEBSITE FOR MORE TEACHER RESOURCES INCLUDING DOL BUNDLE # 1:

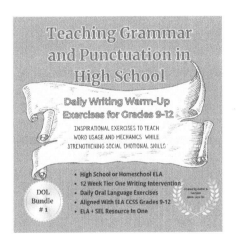

WWW.ANAMCARACAT.COM

LOOKING FOR FREE INSPIRATIONAL WRITING WARM-UPS FOR THE YEAR?

Visit my website to download your free e-book:

Birdseed: A Guide to Teaching Emotional Intelligence in the Primary and Secondary Classroom

WWW.ANAMCARACAT.COM

Also available in paperback on Amazon.

Birdseed is:

- endorsed by the MTSS coordinator for The Colorado Department of Education

- endorsed by New York Times best-selling author and positive psychology expert Shawn Achor

- a tier one MTSS intervention

- a quick, powerful, and inspirational bell-ringer that will transform your classroom atmosphere

A QUICK WORD FROM THE AUTHOR

Aloha, Good People.

As I write this introduction, I am currently living on the beautiful island of Maui, where I also have the privilege of teaching high school students in a private academy.

I started creating DOL for my secondary students nearly 15 years ago because it was overwhelmingly obvious that high school students need direct instruction in grammar and mechanics. They simply don't remember learning these writing skills in primary school, and in truth, they feel insecure for not knowing how to use words and punctuation correctly.

It's not fair to the students to expect them to learn grammar and mechanics in the context of their other writing assignments. They won't simply "pick up the skills" by osmosis. They need DAILY DIRECT INSTRUCTION. Believe it or not, students actually enjoy and appreciate the daily DOL exercises because they are well aware that they don't know the rules of writing, and they genuinely want to learn.

Recently, after completing one of the DOL exercises, one of my 11th grade students said to me, "Kumu (the Hawaiian term for teacher), why has no one taught us this stuff before?" (He was especially grateful to learn how to use the plural possessive apostrophe.) I explained that he likely had been taught the rules of grammar and punctuation in elementary school, but unfortunately it's a challenge to really take in and retain that information at such a young age. High school students' brains are more developed and better able to understand and remember such instruction, so it makes perfect sense to revisit the rules of writing in secondary school.

As a passionate advocate for addressing the social-emotional domain in the classroom, I decided to embed inspirational, life-skills-oriented material within the DOL exercises. Whether or not you take the time to discuss the day's DOL after making the necessary corrections, students are exposed to the optimistic content embedded within each paragraph, and this makes students enjoy the activity even more.

There are many ways to teach grammar and mechanics, and there are countless resources on the market, so I appreciate you trusting me and investing your money in this product. The daily DOL activity is quite simple, but it's extraordinarily effective, and that's why I decided many years ago to start sharing these original resources with other educators. I trust you and your students will find this tool engaging and effective, and I welcome you to email me if you have questions.

Ever your anam cara (Celtic term for soul-friend),
Cat

Table of Contents:

BONUS MINI-LESSONS: Pages 75-95

I've added 16 supplemental mini-lessons to clarify commonly misunderstood grammar and punctuation. When necessary, you can review a term prior to correcting the day's DOL paragraph.

The mini-lessons address:

- clauses, apostrophes, semi-colons, colons, conjunctions, subordinating conjunctions, correlative conjunctions, prepositions, and commonly confused homonyms

Prefer the Digital Version of this Resource?

While you can certainly make hard copies of these pages for your students, you might prefer the digital version to save on paper, to display on the whiteboard, to share with students remotely, or simply to print pages as needed.

Included with your purchase is the option to download this resource as a PDF or Google Doc.

You can instantly download your free version of this DOL bundle by:
1. visiting my website at www.anamcaracat.com
2. adding the resource to your shopping cart and entering the code: **FREEDOLDOC** at checkout (all one word in caps).

My ASK: After looking over the material, I ask that you please take a moment to leave a review on this product. On average, less than 10% of buyers take a moment to do this. I know you're busy, and that's one reason I created this product–to save you time. Your product review helps me to reach more educators and allows me to continue sharing my work to make teachers' lives easier and students' lives better.

As a thank-you for shopping with me, please use coupon code **SAVETEN** towards a resource of your choice on my website;
no minimum purchase is required.

Message to Teachers and Homeschooling Heroes,

Thank you for purchasing this resource!

Daily warm-ups or bell-ringers provide structure and predictability for students, which helps tremendously with behavior management. The first few minutes of class sets the tone for the remainder of the period, so having a *meaningful* daily activity to begin class sets the stage for success.

Also, if you do daily DOL at the start of the class period, your students will be quietly on task while you take attendance. Wouldn't that be dreamy?

Throughout my 13 years in the secondary classroom, I found that *most* students—even the best writers—need DIRECT DAILY INSTRUCTION with grammar and mechanics. Using these DOL paragraphs as part of your daily routine is a quick way to *explicitly* address this skill set that young writers so desperately need! Moreover, because each paragraph is related to personal development, you'll simultaneously be addressing the social-emotional domain, which will keep your students interested and inspired.

The Why and How of Daily DOL:

WHY Daily DOL?

We learn through repetition, and daily DOL warm-ups will significantly improve your students' writing skills! Students rarely receive explicit instruction with grammar and mechanics beyond elementary school, and as secondary teachers we often think they don't need it, or we simply don't have the time to address it in isolation. However, you'll find these daily mini-lessons to be <u>quick</u> and—most importantly—<u>effective</u>!

In addition to strengthening your students' writing skills, these daily mini-lessons allow you to address the social-emotional domain. Regardless of the subjects we teach, we all want our students to be socially and emotionally healthy, but we don't all have the resources or time to teach SEL in isolation. These paragraphs are intended to inspire students and support their metacognitive growth.

PRE-ASSESSMENT:

Sometimes (because they are a bit embarrassed to admit they need this instruction in high school) students initially object to this daily exercise. They might say it's too remedial for them and insist they "already know this stuff." Therefore, to justify doing it as a warm-up every day, and to nip the complaining in the bud, I have students complete the first paragraph independently as a pre-assessment. I tell them, "If you don't need this instruction, show me you don't need it, and we can skip it in the future."

Then I collect them, grade these first paragraphs on my own (I use a quick 1-4 grading scale), **record the grades so I can measure growth throughout the semester/year**, and return them to students. I have NEVER, in my 13 years of teaching high school, found that students *don't* need this daily direct instruction. Upon receiving their graded initial assessments and seeing for themselves how much they need to learn, they will <u>never argue again about doing the daily warm-up. :)</u>

Ongoing Assessments: I use every Friday's DOL as a quiz, and then record those grades so I can monitor growth. On the Monday following the quiz, we review correct answers together. These grades could be considered formative or summative, depending on your grading model. You might consider allowing students to review past DOL exercises or notes during the quizzes.

Introducing DOL to Students:

I use DOL as a daily bell-ringer activity (i.e. the first activity of the day). This creates structure and predictability at the start of every class period, as students know exactly what they should be doing the second they sit down in their seats. While students independently work on DOL for 2-3 minutes, I can take attendance peacefully....It's beautiful.

<u>I introduce the activity by explaining the expected daily procedure. I say:</u>

- We will be doing a quick daily activity at the start of every class period to strengthen your writing skills.

- (Project sample DOL on the whiteboard, hand out paper copies, or share with students via Google Docs and instruct them to open documents so they can see what DOL looks like.)

- When you enter class, you will immediately get out your DOL, which stands for daily oral language, and make corrections to the best of your ability on your own. We will work on one paragraph each day.

- After you have made corrections on your own, I will review the correct answers on the whiteboard.

- At times, I may call upon students to come to the board to make corrections.

- Every Friday, the day's DOL will be considered a quiz and worth [xxxxx] points. Therefore, it's important to pay attention every day that we practice.

I begin the activity by reviewing the What the Heck is a Clause? handout. Then, I give students two minutes to correct a paragraph on their own (one paragraph a day). Then, I make corrections on the board and have them follow along with me to ensure they made all necessary corrections. If they're using paper copies of DOL, I tell them to use a colored pen or highlighter while correcting with me so I can quickly glance at their papers and see what they're getting on their own and what they are needing help with. If they're using Google Docs, I tell them to use a different color highlight when they make corrections with me, again, so I can see what they're able to correct on their own and what they need help with. The first couple of days might take a few minutes longer than usual, but once students get used to the procedure, the entire activity shouldn't take more than six to eight minutes.

*If you have the time, you can use the paragraphs as discussion prompts to generate whole group discussion after the corrections are made. Alternatively, one day you can do DOL corrections and the following day you can have students write a single paragraph response to the DOL they corrected the previous day. This way they have time to genuinely reflect on the messages embedded within each paragraph.

Another idea is to have students come to the board to do the corrections each day. They will need guidance (help from you and/or their classmates), and the activity will take a bit longer, but they love participating, and students always love writing on the board! You can ask for volunteers or pull a name randomly out of a jar. They engage more if they know they may be called upon at some point to do the DOL in front of the class.

If your students are making their initial corrections in a Google Doc, keep in mind that Google Docs will highlight *some* of the grammatical and mechanical errors, but this is okay. Only a few common errors will be highlighted, so there will be plenty of corrections to identify on their own.

The Grammar Game:

After students get the hang of the DOL activity and build up a bit of confidence, you might consider occasionally making a period-long game out of it. I referred to this as The Grammar Game, which we did every other Friday, and kids absolutely loved it! It will take the whole class period, and students can get pretty hyped up, so be sure to set expectations beforehand.

Basically, the game procedure looks like this:
- You split the class into halves.

- You can let each of the two teams decide on a team name, which you will write on the board for score-keeping.

- You project the DOL onto the whiteboard.

- A person from team one comes to the board to make corrections to one full paragraph, and their peers on their team can help as much as needed. (You may need to set a time limit to keep them from taking too long to make the corrections.)

- Meanwhile team two is quietly making corrections to the same paragraph via their papers or Google Docs (but not helping team one).

- Once team one thinks they've made all the necessary corrections on the whiteboard, and they tell me they're done, I say, "Okay, final answer?"

- Once team one says, "Yes, final answer," I turn to team two and ask them if team one missed anything: "Did they miss any corrections that still need to be made, or did they make any mistakes with their corrections?"

- If team two doesn't catch any missed corrections or mistakes, then team one gets a point on the board under their team name.

- If team two *does* identify a mistake that team one overlooked, they get the point on the board and team one gets no points that round.

- Be sure to do the final review orally and bring their attention to anything both teams missed. It's up to you if you want to give points when both teams fail to make a necessary correction. For example, if team one didn't add a necessary comma but team two didn't notice, then you may still give team one a point for the round, or you may say no one gets the point because neither team made the necessary correction.

- Then the procedure switches, and someone from team two will come to the board to make corrections with the help of their peers.

- Meanwhile team one will quietly work on the same paragraph via their papers or Google Docs.

- So on and so forth....

Again, the grammar game is an incredibly engaging activity, and the kids can get overly-enthusiastic/competitive about the game, so be sure to set expectations for noise levels and behaviors. You might also consider offering an incentive of some sort to the winning team, but even if they are just playing for the sake of winning, they honestly love this game. What's even better is that they are LEARNING while they are having fun!

What the Heck is a Clause?

And, what's the difference between an independent and a dependent clause?

A clause has a subject and a verb.   *There are two types of clauses:*

1. **Independent Clause** (IC) = complete sentence *(has a subject + verb and makes sense on its own)*
   Example: The fish swam in the river.

2. **Dependent Clause** (DC) = incomplete sentence *(has a subject + verb BUT does not make sense on its own)*
   Example: When the fish swam in the river.

If a sentence begins with a dependent clause and ends with an independent clause, you'll need to add a comma to separate them.

Example:

When it swam in the river, the fish wiggled its body like a mermaid. **(DC, IC.)**

If a sentence begins with an independent clause and ends with a dependent clause, no comma is necessary.

Example:

The fish wiggled its body like a mermaid when it swam in the river. **(IC DC.)**

If you join two independent clauses, you can connect them with a comma and a conjunction, or you can separate them with a period or semicolon.

Examples:

The fish swam in the river, and it wiggled its body like a mermaid. **(IC, and IC.)**

The fish swam in the river; it wiggled its body like a mermaid. **(IC; iC.)**

The fish swam in the river. It wiggled its body like a mermaid. **(IC. IC.)**

www.anamcaracat.com Copyright © 2022 Anam Cara Cat

DOL: Student Document
Daily Oral Language

Directions: Read the following sentences below, and add the missing punctuation as needed. This includes commas, apostrophes, semicolons, and periods. You will also need to capitalize when necessary and replace incorrectly used homophones. **Homophones** are a type of **homonym** that sound alike but have different meanings and different spellings.

Examples of homophones: their, there, they're, to, two, too, your, you're

1. Within each of the DOL paragraphs you are to correct incorrectly used grammar and add correct punctuation as needed this may sound like a remedial task and you may not think you need this daily practice but research reflects that 95% of high school students still need explicit instruction on how to use commas periods semicolons and apostrophes correctly students are always taught the rules of language in early elementary school but rarely do they receive direct instruction on the topic beyond the sixth grade this is truly a shame because when we are older it is easier to understand how to use grammar and punctuation correctly consider this first paragraph as an assessment and a opportunity to show me what you know every students quiz will reflect what they need to work on and Im confident this daily exercise will improve all of my students writing skills please do your best!

2. In addition to teaching you the rules of grammar and mechanics the daily DOL paragraphs are designed to foster metacognition metacognition refers to thinking about the way you think the daily DOL will inspire you to reflect on your thought patterns and beliefs thousands of thoughts are floating through your mind everyday but do they serve or disempower you its important to assess the condition of your mindset because how you think effects how you feel and how you feel effects how you behave ultimately your behavior affects the quality of your life so positive life changes must begin at the root with positive changes in thinking.

3. Its important to remember that the thoughts we think over and over again eventually become beliefs this can work to ones benefit or to ones demise for example if you repeatedly tell yourself that your a dedicated student and your grades are important to you eventually you will begin to believe this and this belief will be reflected in your behaviors and positive performance conversely if you repeatedly tell yourself you suck at school and academics just arent your thing you will eventually embrace this as truth and it will be reflected in your behaviors and poor performance ultimately its important to remember that you shouldnt believe everything you think especially if those thoughts arent serving you in a healthy way.

4. One way you can be mindful of your thoughts is to identify and reflect on the labels youve chosen to embody to often people

allow self-imposed labels to limit there potential for example if you label yourself as a shy person you may always avoid meeting new people or participating in social events because subconsciously youve decided those arent things your capable of doing your more complex then you think and your personality preferences and comfort levels can change as you grow as a person inspirational author and personal development leader wayne dyer once said examine the labels you apply to yourself every label is a boundary or limit you will not let yourself cross.

5. Metaphorically speaking the world is your stage if you want to reinvent your role in life and make positive changes you must first identify whats not working what are some of your present behaviors beliefs and habits that are keeping you from living a happier and healthier life are there people in your social circle that influence you in negative ways what labels have you adopted that limit your growth and potential once youve acknowledged whats not working in your life your able to start recreating your role and rewriting your script the great playwright william shakespeare once said all the worlds a stage and a man in his life plays many parts.

6. Once youre clear about whats not working in your life imagine what your ideal life would look and feel like what matters to you most and how can your life be an outward expression of your deepest values what brings you joy and peace what

makes you feel purposeful what types of people do you most enjoy being around what would your perfect environment look and feel like when thinking about your ideal life it might be easier to start by visualizing your ideal day imagine your perfect morning afternoon and evening where would you be what would you be doing who would you be with and how would you feel.

7. When talking about happiness its important to recognize that happiness and pleasure are not the same thing pleasure is often described as a momentary feeling thats influenced by the senses and caused by an external experience that triggers dopamine production in the brain for example eating your favorite foods listening to your favorite song getting a A on your exam or winning a game can all bring about temporary feelings of pleasure happiness on the other hand tends to be a more stable and long lasting state of peace calm and well being serotonin is the neurotransmitter most often associated with long lasting feelings of happiness.

8. If you unexpectedly won a million dollars tomorrow youd probably feel ecstatic and think your life was forever going to feel blissful however eventually the thrill of being rich would wear off and at some point youd probably end up feeling just as you did before you won the million dollars this doesnt mean money isnt a great thing money can be a fantastic thing and if used wisely it can change peoples lives for the better its just

important to remember that money alone cannot sustain long term happiness some of the most successful and wealthy people in the world became rich because they were happy to begin with and then made a plan to accumulate wealth in fact a man by the name of napoleon hill wrote a book about this very subject hill claims that a happy person is more likely to become rich than an unhappy person and he has the research to prove it could this be true.

9. In 1937 a man by the name of napoleon hill published a book titled think and grow rich this book which has sold over 100 million copies since publication reveals the secrets to attaining unlimited wealth before writing this renowned book hill spent many years studying over five hundred self made millionaires to learn there secrets to success many modern day millionaires attribute their fortunes to the wisdom found within think and grow rich one of the best ways to learn anything is to learn from people who have already mastered the very thing you want to learn therefore if you have any interest in becoming rich why not learn from those who are wealthy it certainly couldnt hurt.

10. Hills book is centered around 13 core principals that are intended to teach you how to unleash the power of your mind and tap into what hill refers to as Infinite Intelligence according to the author once you rewire your brain by creating a habit of positive thinking you can tap into Infinite Intelligence which will

intuitively guide you to achieve your greatest goals the problem with most people according to hill is that they have developed powerful habits of negative thinking and there negative thinking patterns sabotage their chances at success.

11.   Although hills book is mainly about attracting monetary wealth the principles he outlines apply to achieving any goal in life so even if you have no interest in becoming rich his book is a valuable read throughout think and grow rich hill emphasizes that the state or quality of ones life is a direct reflection of the state or quality of ones thoughts for example he says that people that believe life is meaningless and horrible will undoubtedly and repeatedly find themselves in situations and circumstances that reinforce the belief that life is meaningless and horrible conversely people who believe life is miraculous and wonderful will undoubtedly and repeatedly find themselves in situations and circumstances that reinforce the belief that life is miraculous and wonderful according to hill we attract what we think about most what do you think about most this might give you an example that supports or refutes hills perspective.

12.   According to napoleon hill the first step to achieving wealth or anything else in life for that matter is to have a very clear idea of what you desire many people say they want to be rich but few people take the time to imagine exactly what that would look and feel like in there lives what would being rich

look and feel like for you how much money would you have to have in order to feel wealthy what would you do with your wealth who would benefit from your wealth these are simple questions but knowing the answers to these questions will allow you to gain clarity if you dont know exactly what you want how can you expect to get it if you dont know *why* you want what you want you wont be motivated to pursue it spend some time visualizing or imagining what wealth would look and feel like in youre life.

13. Hills second principal for attracting wealth is to have unwavering faith that your desire is attainable if your faith is weak then your motivation will be weak and you will not do what must be done in order to turn your dream into a reality this principle applies to achieving any goal in life for example if you want to become a professional athlete and believe that its possible you will practice faithfully every single day in order to strengthen your skills if you want to become a professional athlete but *dont* really believe its possible you wont bother practicing everyday what would be the point one way to strengthen your faith is to spend time everyday visualizing how it would feel to accomplish your goal imagine how your life would change and imagine how other peoples lives would change for the better as well the more you do this the easier it will be to remain faithful to your desire despite challenges or setbacks.

14.   Napoleon hills third principle for attracting wealth is to become conscious of your self-talk and vigilantly guard against negative or self sabotaging thoughts we all talk to ourselves in our heads this is natural the problem is many people say negative and self defeating things on repeat all day every day the more you say something to yourself the more you believe it a repeated thought becomes a habituated thought and a habituated thought becomes a belief your beliefs are then reflected in your actions remember this your thoughts effect your feelings and your feelings influence your actions if you want to change whats happening on the outside you have to change whats happening on the inside your self talk is programming your mind to think negatively or positively.

15.   One way to create a habit of healthy self-talk is to consistently affirm to yourself that you will achieve your goal remind yourself everyday that you are on a mission and you fully intend to see your desire come to fruition speak to yourself as you would to a best friend that is trying to achieve something important you wouldnt say discouraging or hurtful things to your best friend so why would you do that to yourself encourage yourself on a daily basis to stay committed and remind yourself daily of the rewards you will reap by remaining motivated and faithful the more frequently you repeat positive affirmations the more quickly they take root in the subconscious mind the subconscious is where you store your deepest beliefs and your beliefs are the driving force in your everyday life

rewiring the brain through repetition can be very effective.

16. The strategy of employing positive self-talk is called auto-suggestion and it's basically a form of self hypnosis using auto-suggestion to reprogram the subconscious mind through repetition is a psychological technique developed by emile coue at the beginning of the 20th century in addition to mindfully constructing positive self talk during the day hill also suggests listening to positive affirmation audio tracks while sleeping when the mind is at rest it is more susceptible to suggestion and many believe auto-suggestion that occurs during sleep is significantly more effective then self-talk employed during waking hours one way to do this is to record your own voice affirming the completion of your goals or the attainment of your desires then allow the recording to play on repeat as you sleep another way to do this is to simply listen to a positive affirmation video from YouTube while sleeping the affirmations will eventually take hold in your subconscious and become empowering beliefs that positively effect your behavior.

17. Hills fourth principle to attract wealth involves acquiring specialized knowledge in ones field of interest he says that wealthy people are ambitious people who commit to becoming lifelong learners they continuously learn about their fields of interest so as to become authorities in the related subjects Hill claims that people only learn general knowledge in

school but specific and specialized knowledge is more valuable once you decide on your ideal profession you must read books attend seminars and research the related topics he says its also important to form a mastermind group wherein you can associate with others who have similar goals people that work with others toward a common goal tend to achieve success faster then those working alone.

18. According to napoleon hill the fifth strategy for attracting wealth is to passionately engage the imagination hill emphasizes that limitations only exist in the mind and a idea that will lead to riches must be allowed to grow beyond all limitations there must be no room for doubt or negative thinking moreover hill differentiates between what he refers to as "synthetic imagination" and "creative imagination" he explains that synthetic imagination is derived from using and rearranging old ideas creative imagination on the other hand is derived from what he refers to as "Infinite Intelligence" he says that ideas from Infinite Intelligence come in the form of intuition or hunches and this is the creativity that leads to incredible riches allow inspiration to guide you and remember that every great accomplishment started in the imagination as a great idea.

19. The sixth wealth-generating principle outlined in the book think and grow rich is to create a specific plan for action without a plan a goal is just a hope and success isnt built on

hope its built on action you must also keep in mind that your plan and action steps may change as you go and this is to be expected you cant possibly anticipate every challenge so you need to remain flexible and be prepared to adjust action steps as you go persistence is key hill says that many people give up on their dreams just before they are realized.

20.   Napoleon hills seventh step to growing rich is to master procrastination after interviewing hundreds of wealthy people hill shared that one important characteristic all wealthy people had in common was an ability to make decisions quickly and a tendency to change there minds slowly he concluded that a lack of decision making is a major cause of failure for many people a common reason people procrastinate and are unable to make a definite decision is because they are overly concerned with the opinions of others they are afraid of being ridiculed or misunderstood and often find it easier to make no decision rather then make a decision that will be criticized by others therefore the ability to make a decision quickly requires one to think independently and act courageously.

21.   The eighth key to becoming rich according to napoleon hill is persistence a lack of persistence is a major cause of failure and to many people give up on their goals to soon the key to resisting the urge to give up when things get tough is to *remember the reason* you want to accomplish your goal if you dont have a good enough reason to achieve something then

your desire will be weak and if your desire is weak your willpower will be weak as well therefore you must have a good reason to reach your goal and this will motivate you when your faced with challenges you must also remind yourself daily of the benefits you will reap once your goal is accomplished.

22.   The ninth step toward riches is to create a mastermind group which as hill explains is a group of people who will support and encourage you along your journey to success your mastermind group will involve people that can contribute knowledge inspiration and effort toward achieving a common interest people in your mastermind group may have different strengths and different perspectives but they will all have a common goal and this sort of alliance creates a powerful driving force your mastermind group may only involve one or two other people and thats okay the size of the group is not as important as having a common goal and working in harmony to achieve that goal.

23.   The tenth step to accumulating wealth is to program the subconscious mind to operate from a place of positivity and empowerment the subconscious mind is hundreds of times more powerful then the conscious mind and to understand the difference between the two imagine an iceberg in the middle of the ocean you only see a small portion of the iceberg resting above the oceans surface and this bit represents the conscious mind but the majority of the iceberg exists beneath the surface

and this bit represents the subconscious mind the subconscious stores ones deepest beliefs memories and feelings and it influences the majority of ones everyday behaviors unfortunately the information stored in the subconscious mind is not always helpful healthy or even true but it is nonetheless extremely powerful.

24. Disempowering negative and unhealthy beliefs are often stored in the subconscious mind and they influence every aspect of ones life whether they realize it or not how exactly do you know if negative subconscious beliefs are influencing you and affecting your quality of life well step back and take an honest look at your life are you making good choices are you happy do you have a healthy sense of self-esteem are you creating and achieving goals are you living with integrity do you feel a sense of purpose if the answer to any of these questions is no then its entirely possible you have some disempowering or negative subconscious beliefs that need to be addressed there are literally thousands of resources on the market today to help people reprogram their subconscious minds for success and happiness if this topic interests you then do some research read some books on the topic or watch some YouTube videos the information is out there and what you do with it is up to you.

25. Take an inventory of your daily thought patterns assign a percentage to your negative and positive thoughts for

example do you think positively 60% of the time and negatively 40% of the time do negative or positive thoughts dominate your mind in his book think and grow rich napoleon hill writes positive and negative emotions cannot occupy the mind at the same time one or the other must dominate it is your responsibility to make sure that positive thoughts and emotions constitute the dominating influence of your mind.

26. Napoleons hills eleventh step to riches involves expanding your mind and feeding your brain with new information hill recommends hanging out with and learning from people who are smarter then you if you always hang around people who know exactly what you know you will never learn anything new hill compares the brain to a broadcasting station and says that being around intelligent ambitious positive people will make you more intelligent ambitious and positive do you think this could be true hill also recommends reading books that challenge you to think in ways youve never thought before and this includes books that make you question what you already believe remember not everything you believe is true.

27. The twelfth step in hills book is to cultivate and embrace your sixth sense everyone is familiar with the five senses but some people doubt there is such a thing as a sixth sense which might be more easily understood and described as intuition according to hill when one has disciplined their mind to think positively and has developed the habit of taking daily actions

toward a goal the sixth sense will become strengthened this internal insight will act as a guiding light on ones path toward success hill emphasizes that the previous steps must be practiced before one can confidently trust his or her gut.

28. There is more to napoleon hills book think and grow rich and if the aforementioned twelve steps spark your interest you might consider reading his entire text which is available online and anywhere books are sold many modern-day millionaires swear by the principals in hills book but remember the principles relate to success and happiness in general not just monetary wealth therefore it might be worth reading even if you have no interest in becoming rich.

29. Theres another incredibly inspiring book called the magic of thinking big by david schwartz hence the title the book is about thinking big and the seemingly magical results of such thinking schwartz begins his book by emphasizing the importance of having a positive mindset and believing in yourself everyone wants to be successful but few people actually believe they can achieve there goals this is why so many people appear to be simply existing instead of passionately living there lives if you want to live a extraordinary life you cant passively sleepwalk through your days hoping something magical will happen to you you have to make conscious choices that align with your

vision of a fulfilling life it doesnt happen by accident.

30. In his book the magic of thinking big schwartz shares some
     simple strategies for reprogramming ones mind for success he
     suggests that its far easier to replace negative thoughts with
     positive ones than it is to eliminate negative thoughts
     altogether its normal for negative thoughts to come to mind so
     trying to block or deny them is a waste of energy its much more
     effective to simply notice the thoughts that dont feel good and
     then make a deliberate decision to replace them with happy
     thoughts.

31. Within his book Schwartz also emphasizes the importance of
     eliminating excuses that lead to failure successful people make
     a habit of taking action and working through challenges
     whereas unsuccessful people make a habit of making excuses
     and giving up when faced with obstacles everyone that has
     ever achieved anything has had to work through challenges
     thats just a part of the journey toward success its also what
     makes success so rewarding rather then making excuses make
     a plan a very detailed plan the more precise your plan for
     success the less likely it is you will be derailed or discouraged by
     setbacks.

32. Within the book the magic of thinking big there is a chapter
     titled how to turn defeat into victory within this chapter
     Schwartz explains that weve all been wounded in one way or

another weve all felt betrayed abandoned or broken at some point in our lives but the key is not to give up and give in to the story of defeat people have a habit of telling there stories of defeat over and over again until thats the only story they know they start to identify with the sad story and they embrace the role of the victim once youve identified with being a victim it becomes difficult to live the story of the hero or heroine playing the victim has its advantages for example if your story is sad enough it might serve as a good excuse not to create and achieve goals but ultimately embracing the role of the victor is far more beneficial and fulfilling.

33. In Schwartzs chapter titled manage your environment he discusses the powerful influences of ones surroundings one of the most influential elements of ones environment is other people the company you keep contributes to the shaping of who you become for example if you have prolonged associations with pessimistic and apathetic people you will develop behaviors that reflect pessimism and apathy likewise if you have prolonged associations with optimistic and ambitious people you will develop behaviors that reflect optimism and ambition metaphorically speaking if you want to climb to the top of a mountain you dont want to be tied to people who are headed down the mountain.

34.　In Schwartzs chapter titled use goals to help you grow the author emphasizes the importance of goal setting and suggests dividing goals into three categories work home and social in the work category schwartz recommends creating a ten year plan and having goals as they relate to income responsibility and prestige be sure to write down specific goals how much money do you want to be earning ten years from now where is your ideal location for work what type of position will you hold within your chosen profession answering these questions can help you create specific goals with a timeline.

35.　In regards to goals related to home Schwartz says to consider your standards of living as they relate to your house your family and your extracurricular activities what kind of house do you want to live in and where do you want children if so what type of financial support do you want to be able to provide for them what kind of opportunities do you want to offer them what kind of vacations do you want to take and where how often do you want to be able to take holidays.

36.　When creating goals as they relate to your social life Schwartz suggests considering the types of friends you want to have the types of groups you want to belong to and the types of causes you want to support the people you associate with the most will have a tremendous influence on your quality of life therefore its important to choose your friends wisely likewise the social groups you join will influence you and your outlook on life your time is precious so you want the people you spend it with to influence you in a positive and healthy manner when your clear on your values and what matters most to you you will be able to decide what types of causes are worth your time and attention.

37. Creating goals is easy but following through with them can be challenging if you dont have supportive habits in place first of all its important to write down your goals having a goal in your head is not as effective as writing it down in fact studies have shown that people that write down there goals are 85% more likely to achieve them then people who merely have goals in their heads author Brian Tracy has been quoted as saying goals that are not written down are just wishes.

38. As your writing down your goals be sure to be very specific vague goals are of very little use because they cant be measured for example if you have the goal to improve in school you have to know exactly what you want that to look like otherwise how will you know if youve achieved your goal if you want to get better grades be specific about the grades you want to earn and the subjects to which those grades will apply if you want to improve your relationships with teachers or peers be specific about the types of behaviors you intend to change the more specific you are with your intentions the easier it will be to measure your progress.

39.   once you have written down your goals be sure to attach a timeline to them goals without deadlines are much less likely to be achieved creating an end date for your goals creates a sense of urgency which will motivate you to stay on schedule and follow through with youre commitment in addition to having an end goal with a deadline be sure to create smaller goals that serve as stepping stones and attach timelines to those smaller goals as well for example if your long term goal is to save five thousand dollars by the end of your senior year in high school be sure to create short term deadlines such as saving 200 per week that will help you reach your end goal.

40.   Once you have specific goals written down with timelines attached to them be sure to revisit those goals on a daily basis otherwise you might forget about them and if you dont remember your goals your definitely never going to achieve them rather than just looking at your written goals everyday some success gurus suggest *rewriting* the same long term goals day after day this keeps them in the forefront of your mind which will keep you motivated and on track to complete them

41.   in addition to writing down your goals everyday you might consider creating a visual representation of your goals which you can spend time looking at each day as well some people refer to this as a vision board but whatever you want to call it its basically a collage of images that represent what you want to do have and be this is a fun and creative project that can help

you more easily visualize your ideal future there are thousands of articles and videos online about vision boards so if this interests you and you want some ideas just do a quick internet search many successful millionaires claim they used vision boards to achieve there goals.

42.   Another helpful strategy for achieving your goals is to remember the reason you want to achieve them in the first place the stronger your reason for wanting to achieve something the more motivated you will be to follow through with your goal for example if your a entrepreneur that has the goal of working for yourself get clear about *why* you want to work for yourself what are the benefits to being self employed what are the drawbacks to working for other people how would your life and the lives of others change for the better if you were your own boss write down the answers to these questions as a reminder to yourself this will help you to stay inspired jack canfield author of the chicken soup for the soul book series once said people who dont have goals work for people who do.

43.   While pursuing your goals however worthy they may be its important to remember that youre happiness should not be dependent on your achievements Shawn Achor author of the new york times best selling book titled the happiness advantage emphasizes that happiness is the foundation for lasting success not the result of it he says that most people

have a backwards understanding of how happiness works most people believe they can only be happy *after* theyve achieved there goals but that sort of happiness is shallow and short lived the key to both happiness and success is to prioritize your happiness first then you will naturally become more successful in other words success is the result of happiness not the cause of happiness.

44. According to shawn achor and many other authorities in the field of psychology and neuroscience there are several advantages to being happy in addition to generally being more successful happy people tend to be healthier more creative more productive and better problem solvers they also tend to be easier to get along with which opens up more possibilities for them in both their personal and vocational realms because of their strong interpersonal skills happy people are able to establish deeper social bonds and strong social bonds are scientifically proven to lengthen ones lifespan.

45. Within his book Achor emphasizes that happiness is a choice and a habit he says that people must make daily conscious decisions to support the state of happiness and the general feeling of well being he shares multiple strategies that anyone can employ to develop the habit of happiness one of the easiest ways to do this is to adopt an attitude of gratitude by doing daily gratitude exercises Achor suggests writing down at least three things you are genuinely grateful for on a daily basis he challenges readers to do this for 21 consecutive days and

claims that in doing so a person will rewire their brain to operate from a more positive perspective neuroscientists know that the brain can be rewired and this is referred to as neuroplasticity.

46.   Another daily happiness exercise that Achor recommends is 15 minutes of a fun cardio activity this can be dancing walking skating or whatever brings you joy while also increasing your heart rate the important thing is that you find the activity enjoyable if you dont look forward to doing it youll procrastinate and find excuses not to exercise most people know that physical activity is good for the bodys muscles and bones but its also good for cognitive health people who exercise regularly tend to have better focus better memory and better problem solving skills they also enjoy a state of healthy emotional balance.

47.   Another happiness exercise achor shares in his book the happiness advantage is to perform intentional acts of kindness on a daily basis when we make others feel good we feel good in return and this is a feeling the brain can easily become addicted to obviously you dont want to turn into a obsessive people pleaser and do kind things for the sole purpose of feeling good you want to do mindful acts of kindness that are meaningful to you and the receiver these gestures do not have to be grand they just have to be sincere this can be as simple as making the conscious choice to sincerely thank your bus

driver everyday as your getting off the bus you might unexpectedly do the dishes or make dinner for your parent one evening without being asked you might also do something kind for the planet such as choosing to eat a plant based meal because its more sustainable.

48. Meditation is another daily exercise Achor recommends to support ones level of happiness meditation doesnt have to be complicated or take place in some sacred space nor does it need to be a lengthy ordeal if you want to make meditation a daily habit its best to do it at the same time everyday such as upon awakening in the morning simply take two minutes to focus on your breathing focus on your inhale and then focus on your exhale this simple exercise relaxes your central nervous system and sets a calm tone in your mind and body for the day ahead.

49. Researchers have long known that ones social connections have a powerful impact on his or her overall quality of life including success health and life expectancy therefore spending time with friends and relatives you love is extremely important your brain also releases a hormone and neurotransmitter called oxytocin when your bonding with people and this is one of the reasons time spent with close family and friends feels so good when you prioritize your relationships your simultaneously prioritizing your emotional and

physical health isnt that fantastic.

50.   In one of the final chapters in achors book he discusses the
      ripple effect that happiness has on the people in your life your
      habits attitudes and actions are quite literally contagious and
      spread through a web of social connections if you think about
      it your positive and negative behaviors affect people youve
      never even met for example if youre extremely rude to the
      person bagging your groceries they may in turn get angry and
      then be rude to the next person who comes through their line
      then that person might go home and be rude to her husband
      and children because someone at the grocery spoke to her
      rudely and put her in a bad mood a similar yet more positive
      ripple effect would apply if you were extremely kind to the
      person bagging your groceries when your consistently feeling
      grateful optimistic and happy the people around you feel it to
      your behavior be it positive or negative is infectious so if you
      want to spread positivity be mindful of your attitudes your
      behaviors and your words.

51.   Renowned philosopher and new york times best selling
      author michael singer wrote a book called the untethered soul
      in this book he talks about the pursuit of happiness and explains
      that most people mistakenly believe that happiness can only
      be found outside of themselves most people are convinced
      that a person a thing a place a status or a number in the bank

account is the missing link to there happiness however these external desires only bring momentary happiness and fleeting feelings of well being singer emphasizes that if one wants to experience long lasting joy and peace they have to stop being distracted by external desires and look inward toward the true source of happiness.

52.   So what exactly do philosophers mean when they say happiness is found within it sounds good but how exactly does one look inward for peace and fulfillment according to singer the first step is to make the conscious decision to be happy he basically says that happiness is a choice not a fortuitous accident the second step is to acknowledge that external desires are often just distractions we think that if we get what we want then we can be happy and if we dont get what we want we cant be happy but this is just an erroneous belief system we have been conditioned by society to believe we have to have certain things or look a certain way before we can be happy but this leaves happiness out of our control the truth is happiness is completely within our control and when we recognize this truth everything changes for the better.

53.   Michael singer explains that most people convince themselves that if life is not exactly how they think it *should* be then they cant be happy as a consequence many people are unhappy because much of life is beyond their control a remedy to this limiting perspective is to release expectations

and resistance to what *is* and to practice *observing* rather than *judging* for example if you tell yourself you hate the rain and wake up to see its pouring down outside you make the judgment that the rain is bad you simultaneously make the decision to be unhappy until the sun comes back out an alternative to hating the rain is to simply *observe* that its raining theres no need to judge it as a bad thing or to decide that its going to ruin your day this doesnt mean you have to pretend to love the rain it just means your not allowing your preferences to determine your mood you can accept that its raining and acknowledge that the rain is temporary this may seem like a overly simplified example but think about how it can be applied to your own life what situations are making you unhappy because you are judging them rather than observing them for what they are.

54.   According to Singer If you have decided that your happiness depends solely on getting what you want you create your own suffering what if you want to be in a relationship with a certain person but that person doesnt want to be in a relationship with you does that mean you cant be happy if you want to be a millionaire but you never have a million dollar business idea and never win the lottery does that mean you can never be happy if you hate where you live but are to young to move away on your own does this mean you cant be happy until you move of course there are some external situations you *do* have control over and if you can control them and change them for the

better you should the important thing is to recognize whats within and beyond your control and not to allow what you cant control to determine how you feel.

55. Within his book the untethered soul Michael Singer also addresses the incessant voices we all have talking in our heads we are constantly having conversations with ourselves or having imaginary conversations with other people the quality of these conversations has an enormous influence on how we feel for example if you are constantly lamenting the past criticizing yourself or worrying about the future you will likely feel sad or anxious much of the time conversely if you frequently think about the blessings in your life feel proud of yourself and imagine all the beautiful possibilities that await you you will likely feel peaceful and happy most of the time what is playing on repeat in your own mind are youre thoughts serving you in a healthy way or are they self defeating and exhausting.

56. Just as singer suggests observing rather then judging external circumstances he also suggests observing rather then judging the thoughts in your head he says that people need to make a definite distinction between who they are and what they think this distinction leads to the ultimate state of freedom think about that for a minute you are not your thoughts your thoughts are not you they are simply "recordings" that play on repeat which are based on beliefs or fears you have developed over time once you recognize your thoughts are

separate from you youre better able to control how you feel.

57.   Everyone has a different definition of success its important that you know exactly what success would look and feel like in youre own life its also important to know the difference between achievement and fulfillment achievement refers to accomplishing goals whereas fulfillment refers to feeling joy in the *process* in other words fulfillment is all about the journey not the destination when planning for your future its important to prioritize how you will feel not just what you will do people often feel a deep sense of fulfillment when contributing something of value to the world and some say fulfillment is even more important then happiness what do you think.

58.   If you want to make more time in your life for the things that really matter to you identify the activities that are distracting you and/or draining your attention and energy reflect on a typical day in your life how much time each day do you spend surfing social media watching tv playing video games or participating in some other activity that ultimately feels like a time waster ask yourself are these pastimes moving you closer to your goals or farther away from them how could you spend youre time more wisely every day and how would your life change if you did.

59.   Its easy to focus on all of the bad aspects of life and if you do it often enough it will become a habit once youve made a

habit of focusing on the negatives in life you will become nearly blind to lifes gifts and possibilities please remember how you think affects how you feel and how you feel affects how you behave your behavior will affect your opportunities in life and this will affect your entire life as a whole if you want to be the master of your life instead of a victim of life learn to become a master of your thoughts there are countless books on the market on this very subject the happiest and most successful people in the world have learned skills that allow them to be happy and successful it doesnt happen by accident you have to learn these skills somewhere and books provide a world of knowledge at your fingertips if you dont enjoy reading consider listening to books on audio apps such as audible its never to late or too early to change your thoughts and therefore its never too late to change your life.

60.   While these daily DOL exercises were intended to strengthen your writing skills they were also intended to strengthen your life skills writing well is extremely important because it allows you to communicate more effectively and strong communication skills equate to power in this modern world being self aware and reflecting on your thoughts behaviors and attitudes is also extremely empowering and hopefully you were inspired by the ideas within these exercises.

TEACHER AND STUDENT KEY

DOL

Daily Oral Language

Directions: Read the following sentences below, and add the missing punctuation as needed. This includes commas, apostrophes, semicolons, and periods. You will also need to capitalize when necessary and replace incorrectly used homophones. **Homophones** are a type of **homonym** that sound alike but have different meanings and different spellings.

Examples of homophones: their, there, they're, to, two, too, sea, see

1. Within each of the DOL paragraphs, you are to correct incorrectly used grammar and add correct punctuation as needed. This may sound like a remedial task, and you may not think you need this daily practice, but research reflects that 95% of high school students still need explicit instruction on how to use commas, periods, semicolons, and apostrophes correctly. Students are always taught the rules of language in early elementary school, but rarely do they receive direct instruction on the topic beyond the sixth grade. This is truly a shame because when we are older, it is easier to understand how to use grammar and punctuation correctly. Consider this first paragraph as an assessment and an opportunity to show me what you know. Every student's quiz will reflect what he or she needs to work on, and I'm confident this daily exercise will

improve all of my students' writing skills. Please do your best!

2. In addition to teaching you the rules of grammar and mechanics, the daily DOL paragraphs are designed to foster metacognition. Metacognition refers to thinking about the way you think. The daily DOL will inspire you to reflect on your thought patterns and beliefs. Thousands of thoughts are floating through your mind every day, but do they serve or disempower you? It's important to assess the condition of your mindset because how you think affects how you feel, and how you feel affects how you behave. Ultimately, your behavior affects the quality of your life, so positive life changes must begin at the root with positive changes in thinking.

3. It's important to remember that the thoughts we think over and over again eventually become beliefs. This can work to one's benefit or to one's demise. For example, if you repeatedly tell yourself that you're a dedicated student and your grades are important to you, eventually you will begin to believe this, and this belief will be reflected in your behaviors and positive performance. Conversely, if you repeatedly tell yourself you suck at school and academics just aren't your thing, you will eventually embrace this as truth, and it will be reflected in your behaviors and poor performance. Ultimately, it's important to remember that you shouldn't believe everything you think, especially if those thoughts aren't serving you in a healthy way.

4. One way you can be mindful of your thoughts is to identify and reflect on the labels you've chosen to embody. Too often, people allow self-imposed labels to limit their potential. For example, if you label yourself as a shy person, you may always avoid meeting new people or participating in social events because subconsciously you've decided those aren't things you're capable of doing. You're more complex than you think, and your personality preferences and comfort levels can change as you grow as a person. Inspirational author and personal development leader Wayne Dyer once said, "Examine the labels you apply to yourself. Every label is a boundary or limit you will not let yourself cross."

5. Metaphorically speaking, the world is your stage. If you want to reinvent your role in life and make positive changes, you must first identify what's not working. What are some of your present behaviors, beliefs, and habits that are keeping you from living a happier and healthier life? Are there people in your social circle who influence you in negative ways? What labels have you adopted that limit your growth and potential? Once you've acknowledged what's not working in your life, you're able to start recreating your role and rewriting your script. The great playwright William Shakespeare once said, "All the world's a stage, and a man in his life plays many parts."

6. Once you're clear about what's not working in your life, imagine what your ideal life would look and feel like. What

matters to you most, and how can your life be an outward expression of your deepest values? What brings you joy and peace? What makes you feel purposeful? What types of people do you most enjoy being around? What would your perfect environment look and feel like? When thinking about your ideal life, it might be easier to start by visualizing your ideal day. Imagine your perfect morning, afternoon, and evening. Where would you be? What would you be doing? Who would you be with, and how would you feel?

7. When talking about happiness, it's important to recognize that happiness and pleasure are not the same thing. Pleasure is often described as a momentary feeling that's influenced by the senses and caused by an external experience that triggers dopamine production in the brain. For example, eating your favorite foods, listening to your favorite song, getting an A on your exam, or winning a game can all bring about temporary feelings of pleasure. Happiness, on the other hand, tends to be a more stable and long-lasting state of peace, calm, and well-being. Serotonin is the neurotransmitter most often associated with long-lasting feelings of happiness.

8. If you unexpectedly won a million dollars tomorrow, you'd probably feel ecstatic and think your life was forever going to feel blissful. However, eventually the thrill of being rich would wear off, and at some point you'd probably end up feeling just as you did before you won the million dollars. This doesn't mean

money isn't a great thing. Money can be a fantastic thing, and if used wisely, it can change people's lives for the better. It's just important to remember that money alone cannot sustain long-term happiness. Some of the most successful and wealthy people in the world became rich because they were happy to begin with and then made a plan to accumulate wealth. In fact, a man by the name of Napoleon Hill wrote a book about this very subject. Hill claims that a happy person is more likely to become rich than an unhappy person, and he has the research to prove it. Could this be true?

9. In 1937, a man by the name of Napoleon Hill published a book titled <u>Think and Grow Rich.</u> This book, which has sold over 100 million copies since publication, reveals the secrets to attaining unlimited wealth. Before writing this renowned book, Hill spent many years studying over five hundred self-made millionaires to learn their secrets to success. Many modern-day millionaires attribute their fortunes to the wisdom found within **Think and Grow Rich.** One of the best ways to learn anything is to learn from people who have already mastered the very thing you want to learn. Therefore, if you have any interest in becoming rich, why not learn from those who are wealthy? It certainly couldn't hurt.
[Emphasize to students that book titles can be italicized, underlined, or bolded.]

10.   Hill's book is centered around 13 core principles that are intended to teach you how to unleash the power of your mind and tap into what Hill refers to as "Infinite Intelligence." According to the author, once you rewire your brain by creating a habit of positive thinking, you can tap into Infinite Intelligence, which will intuitively guide you to achieve your greatest goals. The problem with most people, according to Hill, is that they have developed powerful habits of negative thinking, and their negative thinking patterns sabotage their chances at success.

11.   Although Hill's book is mainly about attracting monetary wealth, the principles he outlines apply to achieving any goal in life, so even if you have no interest in becoming rich, his book is a valuable read. Throughout Think and Grow Rich, Hill emphasizes that the state or quality of one's life is a direct reflection of the state or quality of one's thoughts. For example, he says that people who believe life is meaningless and horrible will undoubtedly and repeatedly find themselves in situations and circumstances that reinforce the belief that life is meaningless and horrible. Conversely, people who believe life is miraculous and wonderful will undoubtedly and repeatedly find themselves in situations and circumstances that reinforce the belief that life is miraculous and wonderful. According to Hill, we attract what we think about most. What do you think about most? This might give you an example that supports or refutes

Hill's perspective.

12.   According to Napoleon Hill, the first step to achieving wealth, or anything else in life for that matter, is to have a very clear idea of what you desire. Many people say they want to be rich, but few people take the time to imagine exactly what that would look and feel like in their lives. What would being rich look and feel like for you? How much money would you have to have in order to feel wealthy? What would you do with your wealth? Who would benefit from your wealth? These are simple questions, but knowing the answers to these questions will allow you to gain clarity. If you don't know exactly what you want, how can you expect to get it? If you don't know *why* you want what you want, you won't be motivated to pursue it. Spend some time visualizing or imagining what wealth would look and feel like in your life.

13.   Hill's second principle for attracting wealth is to have unwavering faith that your desire is attainable. If your faith is weak, then your motivation will be weak, and you will not do what must be done in order to turn your dream into a reality. This principle applies to achieving any goal in life. For example, if you want to become a professional athlete and believe that it's possible, you will practice faithfully every single day in order to strengthen your skills. If you want to become a professional athlete but *don't* really believe it's possible, you won't bother practicing every day. What would be the point? One way to

strengthen your faith is to spend time every day visualizing how it would feel to accomplish your goal. Imagine how your life would change, and imagine how other people's lives would change for the better as well. The more you do this, the easier it will be to remain faithful to your desire despite challenges or setbacks.

14. Napoleon Hill's third principle for attracting wealth is to become conscious of your self-talk and vigilantly guard against negative or self-sabotaging thoughts. We all talk to ourselves in our heads; this is natural. The problem is many people say negative and self-defeating things on repeat all day every day. The more you say something to yourself, the more you believe it. A repeated thought becomes a habituated thought, and a habituated thought becomes a belief. Your beliefs are then reflected in your actions. Remember this. Your thoughts affect your feelings, and your feelings influence your actions. If you want to change what's happening on the outside, you have to change what's happening on the inside. Your self-talk is programming your mind to think negatively or positively.

Explain to students that a semicolon has the same power as a period in that it's used to separate two clauses. If the two clauses are very closely related, it may feel more appropriate to use a semicolon (which has a *softer* stop) than a period (which has a *harder* stop). If students used periods instead of semicolons, that is also correct. Be sure to note that if a semicolon is ever used instead of a period, then the following word must not be capitalized.

Examples:
Sara studied late into the night; she was utterly exhausted.
vs.
Sara studied late into the night. She was utterly exhausted.

15.   One way to create a habit of healthy self-talk is to consistently affirm to yourself that you will achieve your goal. Remind yourself every day that you are on a mission, and you fully intend to see your desire come to fruition. Speak to yourself as you would to a best friend who is trying to achieve something important. You wouldn't say discouraging or hurtful things to your best friend, so why would you do that to yourself? Encourage yourself on a daily basis to stay committed, and remind yourself daily of the rewards you will reap by remaining motivated and faithful. The more frequently you repeat positive affirmations, the more quickly they take root in the subconscious mind. The subconscious is where you store your deepest beliefs, and your beliefs are the driving force in your everyday life. Rewiring the brain through repetition can be very effective.

16.   The strategy of employing positive self-talk is called auto-suggestion, and it's basically a form of self-hypnosis. Using auto-suggestion to reprogram the subconscious mind through repetition is a psychological technique developed by Emile Coue at the beginning of the 20th century. In addition to mindfully constructing positive self-talk during the day, Hill also suggests listening to positive affirmation audio tracks while

sleeping. When the mind is at rest, it is more susceptible to suggestion, and many believe auto-suggestion that occurs during sleep is significantly more effective than self-talk employed during waking hours. One way to do this is to record your own voice affirming the completion of your goals or the attainment of your desires; then, allow the recording to play on repeat as you sleep. Another way to do this is to simply listen to a positive affirmation video from YouTube while sleeping. The affirmations will eventually take hold in your subconscious and become empowering beliefs that positively affect your behavior.

17.   Hill's fourth principle to attract wealth involves acquiring specialized knowledge in one's field of interest. He says that wealthy people are ambitious people who commit to becoming lifelong learners. They continuously learn about their fields of interest so as to become authorities in the related subjects. Hill claims that people only learn general knowledge in school, but specific and specialized knowledge is more valuable. Once you decide on your ideal profession, you must read books, attend seminars, and research the related topics. He says it's also important to form a mastermind group, wherein you can associate with others who have similar goals. People who work with others toward a common goal tend to achieve success faster than those working alone.

18.   According to Napoleon Hill, the fifth strategy for attracting wealth is to passionately engage the imagination. Hill emphasizes that limitations only exist in the mind, and an idea that will lead to riches must be allowed to grow beyond all limitations. There must be no room for doubt or negative thinking. Moreover, Hill differentiates between what he refers to as "synthetic imagination" and "creative imagination." He explains that synthetic imagination is derived from using and rearranging old ideas. Creative imagination, on the other hand, is derived from what he refers to as "Infinite Intelligence." He says that ideas from Infinite Intelligence come in the form of intuition or hunches, and this is the creativity that leads to incredible riches. Allow inspiration to guide you, and remember that every great accomplishment started in the imagination as a great idea.

19.   The sixth wealth-generating principle outlined in the book Think and Grow Rich is to create a specific plan for action. Without a plan, a goal is just a hope, and success isn't built on hope. It's built on action. You must also keep in mind that your plan and action steps may change as you go, and this is to be expected. You can't possibly anticipate every challenge, so you need to remain flexible and be prepared to adjust action steps as you go. Persistence is key. Hill says that many people give up on their dreams just before they are realized.

20.　Napoleon Hill's seventh step to growing rich is to master procrastination. After interviewing hundreds of wealthy people, Hill shared that one important characteristic all wealthy people had in common was an ability to make decisions quickly and a tendency to change their minds slowly. He concluded that a lack of decision-making is a major cause of failure for many people. A common reason people procrastinate and are unable to make a definite decision is because they are overly-concerned with the opinions of others. They are afraid of being ridiculed or misunderstood and often find it easier to make no decision rather than make a decision that will be criticized by others. Therefore, the ability to make a decision quickly requires one to think independently and act courageously.

21.　The eighth key to becoming rich according to Napoleon Hill is persistence. A lack of persistence is a major cause of failure, and too many people give up on their goals too soon. The key to resisting the urge to give up when things get tough is to *remember the reason* you want to accomplish your goal. If you don't have a good enough reason to achieve something, then your desire will be weak, and if your desire is weak, your willpower will be weak as well. Therefore, you must have a good reason to reach your goal, and this will motivate you when you're faced with challenges. You must also remind yourself daily of the benefits you will reap once your goal is accomplished.

22.   The ninth step toward riches is to create a mastermind group, which, as Hill explains, is a group of people who will support and encourage you along your journey to success. Your mastermind group will involve people who can contribute knowledge, inspiration, and effort toward achieving a common interest. People in your mastermind group may have different strengths and different perspectives, but they will all have a common goal, and this sort of alliance creates a powerful driving force. Your mastermind group may only involve one or two other people, and that's okay. The size of the group is not as important as having a common goal and working in harmony to achieve that goal.

23.   The tenth step to accumulating wealth is to program the subconscious mind to operate from a place of positivity and empowerment. The subconscious mind is hundreds of times more powerful than the conscious mind, and to understand the difference between the two, imagine an iceberg in the middle of the ocean; you only see a small portion of the iceberg resting above the ocean's surface, and this bit represents the conscious mind, but the majority of the iceberg exists beneath the surface, and this bit represents the subconscious mind. The subconscious stores one's deepest beliefs, memories, and feelings, and it influences the majority of one's everyday behaviors. Unfortunately, the information stored in the subconscious mind is not always helpful, healthy, or even true,

but it is nonetheless extremely powerful.

24.   Disempowering, negative, and unhealthy beliefs are often stored in the subconscious mind, and they influence every aspect of one's life whether he or she realizes it or not. How exactly do you know if negative subconscious beliefs are influencing you and affecting your quality of life? Well, step back and take an honest look at your life. Are you making good choices? Are you happy? Do you have a healthy sense of self-esteem? Are you creating and achieving goals? Are you living with integrity? Do you feel a sense of purpose? If the answer to any of these questions is no, then it's entirely possible you have some disempowering or negative subconscious beliefs that need to be addressed. There are literally thousands of resources on the market today to help people reprogram their subconscious minds for success and happiness. If this topic interests you, then do some research; read some books on the topic, or watch some YouTube videos. The information is out there, and what you do with it is up to you.

25.   Take an inventory of your daily thought patterns. Assign a percentage to your negative and positive thoughts. For example, do you think positively 60% of the time and negatively 40% of the time? Do negative or positive thoughts dominate your mind? In his book **Think and Grow Rich,** Napoleon Hill writes: "Positive and negative emotions cannot occupy the mind at the same time. One or the other must dominate. It is

your responsibility to make sure that positive thoughts and emotions constitute the dominating influence of your mind."

26.   Napoleons Hill's eleventh step to riches involves expanding your mind and feeding your brain with new information. Hill recommends hanging out with and learning from people who are smarter than you. If you always hang around people who know exactly what you know, you will never learn anything new. Hill compares the brain to a broadcasting station and says that being around intelligent, ambitious, positive people will make you more intelligent, ambitious, and positive. Do you think this could be true? Hill also recommends reading books that challenge you to think in ways you've never thought before, and this includes books that make you question what you already believe. Remember, not everything you believe is true.

27.   The twelfth step in Hill's book is to cultivate and embrace your sixth sense. Everyone is familiar with the five senses, but some people doubt there is such a thing as a sixth sense, which might be more easily understood and described as intuition. According to Hill, when one has disciplined his or her mind to think positively and has developed the habit of taking daily actions toward a goal, the sixth sense will become strengthened. This internal insight will act as a guiding light on one's path toward success. Hill emphasizes that the previous steps must be practiced before one can confidently trust his or

her gut.

28.   There is more to Napoleon Hill's book *Think and Grow Rich*, and if the aforementioned twelve steps spark your interest, you might consider reading his entire text, which is available online and anywhere books are sold. Many modern-day millionaires swear by the principles in Hill's book, but remember, the principles relate to success and happiness in general, not just monetary wealth. Therefore, it might be worth reading, even if you have no interest in becoming rich.

29.   There's another incredibly inspiring book called **The Magic of Thinking Big** by David Schwartz. Hence the title, the book is about thinking big and the seemingly magical results of such thinking. Schwartz begins his book by emphasizing the importance of having a positive mindset and believing in yourself. Everyone wants to be successful, but few people actually believe they can achieve their goals. This is why so many people appear to be simply existing instead of passionately living their lives. If you want to live an extraordinary life, you can't passively sleepwalk through your days hoping something magical will happen to you. You have to make conscious choices that align with your vision of a fulfilling life. It doesn't happen by accident.

30.   In his book The Magic of Thinking Big, Schwartz shares some simple strategies for reprogramming one's mind for success. He

suggests that it's far easier to replace negative thoughts with positive ones than it is to eliminate negative thoughts altogether. It's normal for negative thoughts to come to mind, so trying to block or deny them is a waste of energy. It's much more effective to simply notice the thoughts that don't feel good and then make a deliberate decision to replace them with happy thoughts.

31.   Within his book, Schwartz also emphasizes the importance of eliminating excuses that lead to failure. Successful people make a habit of taking action and working through challenges, whereas unsuccessful people make a habit of making excuses and giving up when faced with obstacles. Everyone who has ever achieved anything has had to work through challenges; that's just a part of the journey toward success. It's also what makes success so rewarding. Rather than making excuses, make a plan, a very detailed plan. The more precise your plan for success, the less likely it is you will be derailed or discouraged by setbacks.

32.   Within the book **The Magic of Thinking Big**, there is a chapter titled "How to Turn Defeat Into Victory." Within this chapter, Schwartz explains that we've all been wounded in one way or another. We've all felt betrayed, abandoned, or broken at some point in our lives, but the key is not to give up and give in to the story of defeat. People have a habit of telling their stories of defeat over and over again until that's the only story they

know; they start to identify with the sad story, and they embrace the role of the victim. Once you've identified with being a victim, it becomes difficult to live the story of the hero or heroine. Playing the victim has its advantages. For example, if your story is sad enough, it might serve as a good excuse not to create and achieve goals, but ultimately, embracing the role of the victor is far more beneficial and fulfilling.

33.　In Schwartz's chapter titled "Manage Your Environment," he discusses the powerful influences of one's surroundings. One of the most influential elements of one's environment is other people. The company you keep contributes to the shaping of who you become. For example, if you have prolonged associations with pessimistic and apathetic people, you will develop behaviors that reflect pessimism and apathy. Likewise, if you have prolonged associations with optimistic and ambitious people, you will develop behaviors that reflect optimism and ambition. Metaphorically speaking, if you want to climb to the top of a mountain, you don't want to be tied to people who are headed *down* the mountain.

34.　In Schwartz's chapter titled "Use Goals to Help You Grow," the author emphasizes the importance of goal-setting and suggests dividing goals into three categories: work, home, and social. In the work category, Schwartz recommends creating a ten year plan and having goals as they relate to income, location, and prestige. Be sure to write down specific goals.

How much money do you want to be earning ten years from now? Where is your ideal location for work? What type of position will you hold within your chosen profession? Answering these questions can help you create specific goals with a timeline.

35.   In regards to goals related to home, Schwartz says to consider your standards of living as they relate to your house, your family, and your extracurricular activities. What kind of house do you want to live in and where? Do you want children? If so, what type of financial support do you want to be able to provide for them? What kind of opportunities do you want to offer them? What kind of vacations do you want to take and where? How often do you want to be able to take holidays?

36.   When creating goals as they relate to your social life, Schwartz suggests considering the types of friends you want to have, the types of groups you want to belong to, and the types of causes you want to support. The people you associate with the most will have a tremendous influence on your quality of life. Therefore, it's important to choose your friends wisely. Likewise, the social groups you join will influence you and your outlook on life. Your time is precious, so you want the people you spend it with to influence you in a positive and healthy manner. When you're clear on your values and what matters most to you, you will be able to decide what types of causes

are worth your time and attention.

37.   Creating goals is easy, but following through with them can be challenging if you don't have supportive habits in place. First of all, it's important to write down your goals. Having a goal in your head is not as effective as writing it down. In fact, studies have shown that people who write down their goals are 85% more likely to achieve them than people who merely have goals in their heads. Author Brian Tracy has been quoted as saying: "Goals that are not written down are just wishes."

38.   As you're writing down your goals, be sure to be very specific. Vague goals are of very little use because they can't be measured. For example, if you have the goal to improve in school, you have to know exactly what you want that to look like. Otherwise, how will you know if you've achieved your goal? If you want to get better grades, be specific about the grades you want to earn and the subjects to which those grades will apply. If you want to improve your relationships with teachers or peers, be specific about the types of behaviors you intend to change. The more specific you are with your intentions, the easier it will be to measure your progress.

39.   Once you have written down your goals, be sure to attach a timeline to them. Goals without deadlines are much less likely to be achieved. Creating an end date for your goals creates a sense of urgency, which will motivate you to stay on schedule

and follow through with your commitment. In addition to having an end goal with a deadline, be sure to create smaller goals that serve as stepping stones, and attach timelines to those smaller goals as well. For example, if your long-term goal is to save five thousand dollars by the end of your senior year in high school, be sure to create short-term deadlines, such as saving 200 per week, that will help you reach your end goal.

40.   Once you have specific goals written down with timelines attached to them, be sure to revisit those goals on a daily basis; otherwise, you might forget about them, and if you don't remember your goals, you're definitely never going to achieve them. Rather than just looking at your written goals every day, some success gurus suggest *rewriting* the same long-term goals day after day. This keeps them in the forefront of your mind, which will keep you motivated and on track to complete them.

41.   In addition to writing down your goals every day, you might consider creating a visual representation of your goals, which you can spend time looking at each day as well. Some people refer to this as a "vision board," but whatever you want to call it, it's basically a collage of images that represent what you want to do, have, and be. This is a fun and creative project that can help you more easily visualize your ideal future. There are thousands of articles and videos online about vision boards, so if this interests you and you want some ideas, just do a quick internet search. Many successful millionaires claim they used

vision boards to achieve their goals.

42.   Another helpful strategy for achieving your goals is to remember the reason you want to achieve them in the first place. The stronger your reason for wanting to achieve something, the more motivated you will be to follow through with your goal. For example, if you're an entrepreneur who has the goal of working for yourself, get clear about *why* you want to work for yourself. What are the benefits to being self-employed? What are the drawbacks to working for other people? How would your life and the lives of others change for the better if you were your own boss? Write down the answers to these questions as a reminder to yourself. This will help you to stay inspired. Jack Canfield, author of the *Chicken Soup for the Soul* book series, once said: "People who don't have goals work for people who do."

43.   While pursuing your goals, however worthy they may be, it's important to remember that your happiness should not be dependent on your achievements. Shawn Achor, author of the New York Times best-selling book titled **The Happiness Advantage**, emphasizes that happiness is the foundation for lasting success, not the result of it. He says that most people have a backwards understanding of how happiness works. Most people believe they can only be happy *after* they've

achieved their goals, but that sort of happiness is shallow and short-lived. The key to both happiness and success is to prioritize your happiness first; then, you will naturally become more successful. In other words, success is the result of happiness, not the cause of happiness.

44.   According to Shawn Achor, and many other authorities in the field of psychology and neuroscience, there are several advantages to being happy. In addition to generally being more successful, happy people tend to be healthier, more creative, more productive, and better problem-solvers. They also tend to be easier to get along with, which opens up more possibilities for them in both their personal and vocational realms. Because of their strong interpersonal skills, happy people are able to establish deeper social bonds, and strong social bonds are scientifically proven to lengthen one's lifespan.

45.   Within his book, Achor emphasizes that happiness is a choice and a habit. He says that people must make daily conscious decisions to support the state of happiness and the general feeling of well-being. He shares multiple strategies that anyone can employ to develop the habit of happiness. One of the easiest ways to do this is to adopt an attitude of gratitude by doing daily gratitude exercises. Achor suggests writing down at least three things you are genuinely grateful for on a daily basis. He challenges readers to do this for 21 consecutive days and claims that in doing so, a person will rewire his or her brain to

operate from a more positive perspective. Neuroscientists know that the brain can be rewired, and this is referred to as neuroplasticity.

46.   Another daily happiness exercise that Achor recommends is 15 minutes of a fun cardio activity. This can be dancing, walking, skating, or whatever brings you joy while also increasing your heart rate. The important thing is that you find the activity enjoyable. If you don't look forward to doing it, you'll procrastinate and find excuses not to exercise. Most people know that physical activity is good for the body's muscles and bones, but it's also good for cognitive health. People who exercise regularly tend to have better focus, better memory, and better problem-solving skills; they also enjoy a state of healthy emotional balance.

47.   Another happiness exercise Achor shares in his book The Happiness Advantage is to perform intentional acts of kindness on a daily basis. When we make others feel good, we feel good in return, and this is a feeling the brain can easily become addicted to. Obviously you don't want to turn into an obsessive people-pleaser and do kind things for the sole purpose of feeling good; you want to do mindful acts of kindness that are meaningful to you and the receiver. These gestures do not have to be grand; they just have to be sincere. This can be as simple as making the conscious choice to sincerely thank your bus driver every day as you're getting off the bus. You might

unexpectedly do the dishes or make dinner for your parent one evening without being asked. You might also do something kind for the planet such as choosing to eat a plant-based meal because it's more sustainable.

48.　Meditation is another daily exercise Achor recommends to support one's level of happiness. Meditation doesn't have to be complicated or take place in some sacred space, nor does it need to be a lengthy ordeal. If you want to make meditation a daily habit, it's best to do it at the same time every day, such as upon awakening in the morning. Simply take two minutes to focus on your breathing; focus on your inhale, and then focus on your exhale. This simple exercise relaxes your central nervous system and sets a calm tone in your mind and body for the day ahead.

49.　Researchers have long known that one's social connections have a powerful impact on his or her overall quality of life, including success, health, and life expectancy. Therefore, spending time with friends and relatives you love is extremely important. Your brain also releases a hormone and neurotransmitter called oxytocin when you're bonding with people, and this is one of the reasons time spent with close family and friends feels so good. When you prioritize your relationships, you're simultaneously prioritizing your emotional and physical health. Isn't that fantastic?

50. In one of the final chapters in Achor's book, he discusses the ripple effect that happiness has on the people in your life. Your habits, attitudes, and actions are quite literally contagious and spread through a web of social connections. If you think about it, your positive and negative behaviors affect people you've never even met. For example, if you're extremely rude to the person bagging your groceries, he or she may in turn get angry and then be rude to the next person who comes through his or her line. Then, that person might go home and be rude to her husband and children because someone at the grocery spoke to her rudely and put her in a bad mood. A similar, yet more positive, ripple effect would apply if you were extremely kind to the person bagging your groceries. When you're consistently feeling grateful, optimistic, and happy, the people around you feel it too. Your behavior, be it positive or negative, is infectious, so if you want to spread positivity, be mindful of your attitudes, your behaviors, and your words.

51. Renowned philosopher and New York Times best-selling author Michael Singer wrote a book called *The Untethered Soul*. In this book, he talks about the pursuit of happiness and explains that most people mistakenly believe that happiness can only be found *outside* of themselves. Most people are convinced that a person, a thing, a place, a status, or a

number in the bank account is the missing link to their happiness. However, these external desires only bring momentary happiness and fleeting feelings of well-being. Singer emphasizes that if one wants to experience long-lasting joy and peace, he or she has to stop being distracted by external desires and look inward toward the true source of happiness.

52.   So what exactly do philosophers mean when they say "happiness is found within"? It sounds good, but how exactly does one look inward for peace and fulfillment? According to Singer, the first step is to make the conscious decision to be happy. He basically says that happiness is a choice, not a fortuitous accident. The second step is to acknowledge that external desires are often just distractions. We think that if we get what we want, then we can be happy, and if we don't get what we want, we can't be happy, but this is just an erroneous belief system. We have been conditioned by society to believe we have to have certain things or look a certain way before we can be happy, but this leaves happiness out of our control. The truth is, happiness is completely within our control, and when we recognize this truth, everything changes for the better.

53.   Michael Singer explains that most people convince themselves that if life is not exactly how they think it *should* be, then they can't be happy. As a consequence, many people

are unhappy because much of life is beyond their control. A remedy to this limiting perspective is to release expectations and resistance to what *is* and to practice *observing* rather than *judging*. For example, if you tell yourself you hate the rain and wake up to see it's pouring down outside, you make the judgment that the rain is bad; you simultaneously make the decision to be unhappy until the sun comes back out. An alternative to hating the rain is to simply *observe* that it's raining; there's no need to judge it as a bad thing or to decide that it's going to ruin your day. This doesn't mean you have to pretend to love the rain. It just means you're not allowing your preferences to determine your mood. You can accept that it's raining and acknowledge that the rain is temporary. This may seem like an overly-simplified example, but think about how it can be applied to your own life. What situations are making you unhappy because you are judging them rather than observing them for what they are?

54.   According to Singer, if you have decided that your happiness depends solely on getting what you want, you create your own suffering. What if you want to be in a relationship with a certain person, but that person doesn't want to be in a relationship with you? Does that mean you can't be happy? If you want to be a millionaire, but you never have a million dollar business idea and never win the lottery, does that mean you can never be happy? If you hate where you live but are too young to move away on your own, does this mean you

can't be happy until you move? Of course, there are some external situations you *do* have control over, and if you can control them and change them for the better, you should. The important thing is to recognize what's within and beyond your control and not to allow what you can't control to determine how you feel.

55.   Within his book **The Untethered Soul,** Michael Singer also addresses the incessant voices we all have talking in our heads. We are constantly having conversations with ourselves or having imaginary conversations with other people. The quality of these conversations has an enormous influence on how we feel. For example, if you are constantly lamenting the past, criticizing yourself, or worrying about the future, you will likely feel sad or anxious much of the time. Conversely, if you frequently think about the blessings in your life, feel proud of yourself, and imagine all the beautiful possibilities that await you, you will likely feel peaceful and happy most of the time. What is playing on repeat in your own mind? Are your thoughts serving you in a healthy way, or are they self-defeating and exhausting?

56.   Just as Singer suggests observing rather than judging external circumstances, he also suggests observing rather than judging the thoughts in your head. He says that people need to make a definite distinction between who they are and what they think. This distinction leads to the ultimate state of freedom. Think

about that for a minute. You are not your thoughts. Your thoughts are not you; they are simply "recordings" that play on repeat, which are based on beliefs or fears you have developed over time. Once you recognize your thoughts are separate from you, you're better able to control how you feel.

57. Everyone has a different definition of success. It's important that you know exactly what success would look and feel like in your own life. It's also important to know the difference between achievement and fulfillment. Achievement refers to accomplishing goals, whereas fulfillment refers to feeling joy in the *process*. In other words, fulfillment is all about the journey, not the destination. When planning for your future, it's important to prioritize how you will feel, not just what you will do. People often feel a deep sense of fulfillment when contributing something of value to the world, and some say fulfillment is even more important than happiness. What do you think?

58. If you want to make more time in your life for the things that really matter to you, identify the activities that are distracting you and/or draining your attention and energy. Reflect on a typical day in your life. How much time each day do you spend surfing social media, watching TV, playing video games, or participating in some other activity that ultimately feels like a time-waster? Ask yourself, are these pastimes moving you closer to your goals or farther away from them? How could you spend

your time more wisely every day, and how would your life change if you did?

59.   It's easy to focus on all of the bad aspects of life, and if you do it often enough, it will become a habit. Once you've made a habit of focusing on the negatives in life, you will become nearly blind to life's gifts and possibilities. Please remember, how you think affects how you feel, and how you feel affects how you behave. Your behavior will affect your opportunities in life, and this will affect your entire life as a whole. If you want to be the master of your life, instead of a victim of life, learn to become a master of your thoughts. There are countless books on the market on this very subject. The happiest and most successful people in the world have learned *skills* that allow them to be happy and successful. It doesn't happen by accident. You have to learn these skills somewhere, and books provide a world of knowledge at your fingertips. If you don't enjoy reading, consider listening to books on audio apps, such as Audible. It's never too late or too early to change your thoughts, and therefore it's never too late to change your life.

60.   While these daily DOL exercises were intended to strengthen your writing skills, they were also intended to strengthen your life skills. Writing well is extremely important because it allows you to communicate more effectively, and strong communication skills equate to power in this modern world. Being self-aware and reflecting on your thoughts, behaviors, and attitudes is also extremely empowering, and hopefully you were inspired by the ideas within these exercises.

ELA Standards Aligned With DOL

Language Standard 1 (L.9-10.1 and L.11-12.1):

- Demonstrate command of the conventions of standard English grammar and usage when writing or speaking.
- This standard focuses on students' ability to apply grammar and usage rules in their writing and speaking.

Language Standard 2 (L.9-10.2 and L.11-12.2):

- Demonstrate command of the conventions of standard English capitalization, punctuation, and spelling when writing.
- This standard emphasizes the correct use of capitalization, punctuation marks, and spelling in written work.

Language Standard 3 (L.9-10.3 and L.11-12.3):

- Apply knowledge of language to understand how language functions in different contexts, to make effective choices for meaning or style, and to comprehend more fully when reading or listening.
- This standard encourages students to analyze and understand the use of language in various contexts, which includes examining the role of grammar and punctuation in conveying meaning and style.

Bonus Mini-Lessons:

On the following pages, you'll find 17 supplemental mini-lessons to clarify commonly misunderstood grammar and punctuation. When necessary, you can review a term prior to correcting the day's DOL paragraph.

Contents:

- What the Heck is a Clause?
- What the Heck is an Apostrophe?
- What the Heck is a Semicolon?
- What the Heck is a Colon?
- What the Heck is a Conjunction?
- What the Heck is a Coordinating Conjunction?
- What the Heck is a Subordinate Conjunction?
- What the Heck is a Correlative Conjunction?
- What the Heck is a Preposition?
- It's vs Its
- Everyday vs Every Day
- There vs Their vs They're
- Your vs You're
- Too vs To vs Two
- Then vs Than
- Effect vs Affect
- Lets vs Let's

What the Heck is a Clause?

And, what's the difference between an independent and a dependent clause?

A clause has a subject and a verb. *There are two types of clauses:*

1. **Independent Clause** = complete sentence *(has a subject + verb and makes sense on its own)*
   Example: The fish swam in the river.

2. **Dependent Clause** = incomplete sentence *(has a subject + verb BUT does not make sense on its own)*
   Example: When the fish swam in the river.

If a sentence begins with a dependent clause and ends with an independent clause, you'll need to add a comma to separate them.
Example:
When it swam in the river, the fish wiggled its body like a mermaid. **(DC, IC.)**

If a sentence begins with an independent clause and ends with a dependent clause, no comma is necessary.
Example:
The fish wiggled its body like a mermaid when it swam in the river. **(IC DC.)**

If you join two independent clauses, you can connect them with a comma and a conjunction, or you can separate them with a period or semicolon.

Examples:
The fish swam in the river, and it wiggled its body like a mermaid. **(IC, and IC.)**
The fish swam in the river; it wiggled its body like a mermaid. **(IC; iC.)**
The fish swam in the river. It wiggled its body like a mermaid. **(IC. IC.)**

What the Heck is an Apostrophe?

What is an Apostrophe? An apostrophe (') is a punctuation mark used to indicate either possession (ownership) or the omission of letters or numbers (*omit* means to leave out).

Using Apostrophes for Contractions:

A contraction is a shortened form of a word or group of words, with the omitted (left out) letters replaced by an apostrophe.

> **Examples:**   do not → don't,   I am → I'm   will not → won't

Apostrophes can also be used to replace numbers.

> **Examples:** I love '80s music more than '90s music.

Using Apostrophes to Show Possession (ownership)

To show that something belongs to someone or something, you add an apostrophe followed by the letter 's'.

> **Here are a few examples:**

- The dog's leash was too short for him. (the leash belongs to the dog)
- My neighbor's house is too close to mine. (the house belongs to the neighbor)
- The student's face was shocked when he saw his grade. (the face belongs to the student)

Plural Possessive: If the noun is plural (more than one) and you need to show possession (or ownership) just add an apostrophe <u>after</u> the 's.'

Here are a few examples:

- The dogs' leashes are all too short. (multiple leashes belong to multiple dogs)
- All of my neighbors' houses look the same. (multiple houses belong to multiple neighbors)
- The students' faces were shocked when they heard about the ten page essay. (multiple faces belong to multiple students)

Now, Let's (let us) Practice Using Apostrophes

1. Its been a long time since we've visited grandmas house.

2. All five of the dogs tails were wagging when their owner walked in with bones.

3. I cant believe the kids dont believe in Santa Clause anymore.

4. In the 1800s, peoples life spans were much shorter because of diseases.

5. The black cats kittens were scattered all over the floors of the house.

6. Isnt it amazing how quickly time flies?

7. The chickens behavior was strange when they knew it was going to rain.

8. Jakes bike needs repair; its chain broke yesterday.

9. We cant go to the park today because its raining.

10. The childrens playground is newly renovated.

11. Whos responsible for organizing todays meeting?

12. She said its the best chocolate cake shes ever tasted.

13. The students performances were better this year.

14. The tiny bluebirds nest was found deep in the trees branches.

15. Dont forget to bring your sisters book tomorrow.

16. Next years bus schedule will look exactly the same as this years.

17. The books cover looked boring, so I didnt bother reading it.

18. The skys color changed rapidly when the storm moved in.

19. The boats all docked in the harbor after the coastguards storm warning.

20. This years prom motif is a 1940s theme; last years theme was the 60s era.

ANSWER KEY: Now, let's (let us) Practice Using Apostrophes

1. It's been a long time since we've visited grandma's house.

2. All five of the dogs' tails were wagging when their owner walked in with bones.

3. I can't believe the kids don't believe in Santa Clause anymore.

4. In the 1800s, people's life spans were much shorter because of diseases.

5. The black cat's kittens were scattered all over the floors of the house.

6. Isn't it amazing how quickly time flies?

7. The chickens' behavior was strange when they knew it was going to rain.

8. Jake's bike needs repair; its chain broke yesterday.

9. We can't go to the park today because it's raining.

10. The children's playground is newly renovated.

11. Who's responsible for organizing today's meeting?

12. She said it's the best chocolate cake she's ever tasted.

13. The students' performances were better this year.

14. The tiny bluebird's nest was found deep in the tree's branches.

15. Don't forget to bring your sister's book tomorrow.

16. Next year's bus schedule will look exactly the same as this year's.

17. The book's cover looked boring, so I didn't bother reading it.

18. The sky's color changed rapidly when the storm moved in.

19. The boats all docked in the harbor after the coastguard's storm warning.

20. This year's prom motif is a 1940s theme; last year's theme was the '60s era.

What the Heck is a Semicolon?

A semicolon has the same strength as a period in that it can separate two independent clauses (complete sentences), but think of a semicolon as a "softer" stop. It should only be used when connecting two very closely related sentences. Also, you <u>do not</u> capitalize the first word in the second sentence.

Examples:

Sometimes I eat cake for breakfast; life's too short to eat cereal every day.

I think my cat eats too much; he gets fatter and fatter each day.

I waited too long for the train; now I'm late for work.

In each of the sentences above, a period can be used instead of the semicolon.

Examples using periods instead of semicolons to join two clauses:

Sometimes I eat cake for breakfast. Life's too short to eat cereal every day.

I think my cat eats too much. He gets fatter and fatter each day.

I waited too long for the train. Now I'm late for work.

Instead of using a semicolon or period to separate two independent clauses (complete sentences), a comma and coordinating conjunction can be used.

Coordinating conjunctions include: for, and, nor, but, or, yet, so   (acronym: FANBOYS)

Examples using conjunctions instead of semicolons to join clauses:

I waited too long for the train, so now I'm late for work.

I think my cat eats too much, and he gets fatter and fatter each day.

What the Heck is a Colon?

A colon is a punctuation mark consisting of two dots, one above the other (:). It's primarily used to introduce a list, explanation, or example, or to separate two independent clauses in a sentence where the second clause explains or expands upon the first.

Here are the main uses of a colon:

1. **Introducing a List:** A colon can be used to introduce a list of items.
   Example: "Please bring the following items to the meeting: pen, notebook, and laptop."

2. **Introducing an Explanation or Example:** A colon can precede an explanation or example that elaborates on the preceding statement.
   Example: "She had one passion: traveling."

3. **Separating Independent Clauses:** A colon can separate two independent clauses in a sentence, where the second clause provides further clarification or elaboration on the first.
   Example: "She had a simple philosophy: work hard, play hard."

4. **Introducing a quote:** A colon may be used to introduce a quote if it is preceded by an independent clause (complete sentence).
   Example: Mark Twain said it best: "Worry is simply having faith in the wrong thing."

It's important to note that a colon should be used after a complete sentence, and there should be no space before it but one space after it. Additionally, it's generally not used to introduce a list if the introductory phrase is an incomplete sentence.

What the Heck is a Conjunction?

A conjunction is a part of speech that connects words, phrases, or clauses within a sentence. Conjunctions are used to show relationships between different parts of a sentence, such as similarity, contrast, addition, or cause and effect. There are three main types of conjunctions:

1. **Coordinating Conjunctions:** These connect words, phrases, or independent clauses of equal importance within a sentence. The most common coordinating conjunctions are "for," "and," "nor," "but," "or," "yet," and "so." (acronym: FANBOYS)

2. **Subordinating Conjunctions:** These introduce dependent clauses and establish a relationship between the dependent clause and the independent clause in a complex sentence. Some common subordinating conjunctions include "because," "although," "while," "if," "since," "before," "after," "when," "unless," and "where." For example: "She went to bed after she finished her homework."

3. **Correlative Conjunctions:** These come in pairs and connect similar parts of a sentence. Common correlative conjunctions include "either...or," "neither...nor," "both...and," "not only...but also," "whether...or," and "not...but." For example: "He is both smart and kind."

Understanding conjunctions is essential for building clear and coherent sentences because they help to combine ideas and add flow to your writing.

What the Heck is a Coordinating Conjunction?

Coordinating Conjunctions: These connect words, phrases, or independent clauses of equal importance within a sentence. The most common coordinating conjunctions are "for," "and," "nor," "but," "or," "yet," and "so" (acronym: FANBOYS)

Example of coordinating conjunctions connecting nouns:
Chihuahuas **and** poodles are dogs.

Example of coordinating conjunction connecting verbs:
My feet hurt so bad after the race that I couldn't walk **or** run for days.

Example of coordinating conjunction connecting adjectives:
My puppy's breath smells funky **yet** sweet.

Example of coordinating conjunction connecting noun phrases:
Painting furniture **and** reading books are two of my favorite hobbies.

Example of coordinating conjunction connecting clauses:
I love living in Hawai'i, **and** I love the year-round warmth.

Note, commas are only necessary when connecting two independent clauses:

Example:
The sea turtles in Maui are beautiful, and they are friendly. (a comma separates two independent clauses)

The sea turtles in Maui are beautiful and very friendly. (only one clause—no comma necessary)

My parents are kind, but they are strict. (a comma separates two independent clauses)
My parents are kind but strict. (only one independent clause—no comma)

What the Heck is a Subordinating Conjunction?

Subordinating Conjunctions:

A subordinating conjunction is a type of conjunction that joins a subordinate (dependent) clause to a main (independent) clause, creating a complex sentence.

Some common subordinating conjunctions include "because," "although," "while," "if," "since," "before," "after," "when," "unless," and "where." For example: "She went to bed after she finished her homework."

Here are a few examples of how subordinating conjunctions are used:

1. "Although it was raining, we decided to go for a walk."
   - "Although" is the subordinating conjunction indicating contrast. It joins the dependent clause "Although it was raining" with the independent clause "we decided to go for a walk."

2. "Because I studied hard, I passed the exam."
   - "Because" is the subordinating conjunction indicating cause and effect. It joins the dependent clause "Because I studied hard" with the independent clause "I passed the exam."

3. "If you finish your homework, you can go out to play."
   - "If" is the subordinating conjunction indicating condition. It joins the dependent clause "If you finish your homework" with the independent clause "you can go out to play."

What the Heck is a Correlative Conjunction?

Correlative conjunctions are pairs of words used to connect similar ideas within a sentence. They work in **pairs** to join words, phrases, or clauses that are equal in importance and grammatical structure. Here are some examples:

1. **Both...and:** Used to join two elements.

    - Example: *Both John and Sarah are attending the party.*

2. **Either...or:** Indicates a choice between two options.

    - Example: *You can either go to the concert or stay home.*

3. **Neither...nor:** Indicates that two options are not applicable.

    - Example: *Neither the cat nor the dog is allowed on the couch.*

4. **Not only...but** also: Emphasizes two related ideas.

    - Example: *She is not only intelligent but also creative.*

5. **Whether...or:** Presents two alternatives.

    - Example: *I don't know whether to laugh or cry.*

Correlative conjunctions are used to maintain parallel structure and clarity in writing.

ARE COMMAS REQUIRED?

When joining two independent clauses (complete sentences), you typically need to use a comma before the second clause.
Examples:

- Both John and Sarah are attending the party, but they're arriving separately.
- *You can either go to the concert, or you can stay home.*

If the second clause is *super* short and closely related to the first clause, you *may* choose to omit the comma for stylistic purposes.

Example: Either I can go to the store or you can go.

If there is only one independent clause, no comma is necessary.

Examples:
- Neither the cat nor the dog is allowed on the couch.
- Not only is she intelligent but also creative.
- I have not only spent all my money shopping but also all of my mother's money!

If there are two independent clauses (more than one subject), a comma is necessary.

Examples:
- Not only is **she** intelligent, but **she** is also creative.
- I have not only spent all my money shopping, but **I've** also spent all of my mother's money!

What the Heck is a Preposition?

A preposition is a word that typically comes before a noun (or pronoun) to show its relationship to another word in the sentence. Prepositions often indicate location, direction, time, or the relationship between different elements in a sentence.

Here are a few examples of common prepositions:

1. **In**: The book is in the bag.
2. **On:** The cat is sitting on the table.
3. **At:** We'll meet at the restaurant.
4. **Under:** The keys are under the mat.
5. **Above:** The bird is flying above the clouds.
6. **Between:** She stood between her two friends.
7. **Before:** We need to finish before dinner.
8. **After:** We'll go for a walk after lunch.
9. **During:** I fell asleep during the movie.
10. **With:** I went to the park with my friends.

Prepositions can also be part of longer phrases called **prepositional phrases**, which include the preposition, its object (the noun or pronoun following it), and any modifiers. For example:

- In the park: "In" is the preposition, and "the park" is its object.
- On the table: "On" is the preposition, and "the table" is its object.

Prepositions are essential for indicating relationships in sentences and are used in various contexts in both written and spoken language.

It's vs Its

"It's" and "its" are both pronouns, but they have different uses and meanings:

1. It's: "It's" is a contraction of "it is" or "it has." The apostrophe represents the missing letter(s). So, "it's" always means "it is" or "it has."
   - **Example:** "It's raining outside." (It is raining outside.)
   - **Example:** "It's been a long day." (It has been a long day.)
   - **Example:** "It's a shame the weather is so cloudy because we wanted to sunbathe." (It is a shame…)

2. Its: "Its" is a possessive pronoun, showing ownership or belonging. It indicates that something belongs to or is associated with "it."
   - **Example:** "The cat chased its tail." (The tail belongs to the cat.)
   - **Example:** "The company announced its new product." (The product belongs to the company.)
   - **Example**: The movie lost its charm after I watched it twenty times.

Remembering the difference between "it's" and "its" can be tricky because apostrophes often indicate possession in English. However, "its" is one of the few possessive pronouns that doesn't use an apostrophe.

Everyday vs Every Day

"Everyday" and "every day" may seem similar, but they are used differently in sentences:

1. Everyday (adjective): "Everyday" is an adjective used to describe something that is commonplace, ordinary, or typical. It's a single word modifying a noun.
   - Example: "I wear my everyday shoes to work." (These are the shoes you wear regularly, not special or fancy ones.)
   - Example: "His everyday routine includes going for a jog in the morning." (This refers to his regular, ordinary routine.)

2. Every day (adverbial phrase): "Every day" consists of the word "every" (an adjective) and "day" (a noun), used together as an adverbial phrase to indicate frequency. It means each day or daily.
   - Example: "I exercise every day." (This means you exercise each day, not skipping any.)
   - Example: "She reads the newspaper every day." (She reads the newspaper daily, without fail.)

In summary, "everyday" is an adjective describing something as common or ordinary, while "every day" is an adverbial phrase indicating something that occurs on a daily basis.

Here's a trick to help you remember:
If you can place the word "single" between the words every and day and it makes sense, then it's two words. Here are some examples:
- I eat vegetables every day. (I eat vegetables every **single** day.).
- I wear sunscreen every day. (I wear sunscreen every **single** day.).

If the word "single" doesn't make sense between the words every and day, then it's one word. Here's an example:
- My everyday clothes are casual and comfortable.
  - It wouldn't make sense to say: My every single day clothes are casual and comfortable.

There vs Their vs They're

"There," "their," and "they're" are homophones, which means they sound the same but have different meanings and are used in different contexts:

1. **There:** "There" is an adverb that indicates a place or position. It's used to refer to a location, whether physical or abstract.

   - Example: "The keys are over there." (Referring to a location.)
   - Example: "There is a park near our house." (Referring to the existence or presence of something.)

2. **Their:** "Their" is a possessive determiner, indicating that something belongs to a group of people or things previously mentioned.

   - Example: "Their house is beautiful." (The house belongs to them.)
   - Example: "The students handed in their assignments." (The assignments belong to the students.)

3. **They're:** "They're" is a contraction of "they are." It combines the subject pronoun "they" with the verb "are."

   - Example: "They're going to the movies tonight." (They are going to the movies tonight.)
   - Example: "They're excited about the trip." (They are excited about the trip.)

Remembering the differences:
- "There" indicates a place.
- "Their" indicates possession by a group.
- "They're" is a contraction of "they are."

Your vs You're

"Your" and "you're" are both pronouns, but they are used differently:

1. **Your:** "Your" is a possessive pronoun, indicating that something belongs to the person or group being addressed.
   - **Example:** "I like your hat." (The hat belongs to you.)
   - **Example:** "What's your favorite color?" (Asking about the favorite color belonging to you.)

2. **You're:** "You're" is a contraction of "you are." It combines the subject pronoun "you" with the verb "are."
   - **Example:** "You're going to enjoy the concert." (You are going to enjoy the concert.)
   - **Example:** "You're a talented musician." (You are a talented musician.)

Remembering the differences:
- "Your" indicates possession.
- "You're" is a contraction of "you are."

If you're talking about something belonging to someone, you'd use "your." If you're expressing a state of being or an action, you'd use "you're."

Too vs To vs Two

"Too," "to," and "two" are all homophones, which means they sound the same but have different meanings and are used in different contexts:

1. **Too:** "Too" is an adverb that means "also" or "excessively." It indicates an additional degree or amount.
    - **Example:** "She wanted to come too." (She wanted to come also.)
    - **Example:** "The cake was too sweet." (The cake was excessively sweet.)

2. **To:** "To" is a versatile preposition that has several uses, but primarily it indicates direction, destination, or relation.
    - **Example:** "We went to the park." (Indicating the destination.)
    - **Example:** "She gave the book to him." (Indicating direction or relation.)

3. **Two:** "Two" is a number, specifically the numerical representation of the quantity 2.
    - **Example:** "There are two apples on the table." (Referring to the number of apples.)

Remembering the differences:

- "Too" means "also" or "excessively."
- "To" is a preposition indicating direction, destination, or relation.
- "Two" is the number 2.

Then vs Than

"Then" and "than" are both commonly used words in English, but they have different meanings and functions:

1. **Then:** "Then" is an adverb used to indicate time or sequence. It can also be used to express a consequence or result.
   - **Example:** "We went to the store, and then we went to the park." (Indicating sequence or order of events.)
   - **Example:** "If you finish your homework, then you can go outside to play." (Indicating a consequence or result.)

2. **Than:** "Than" is a conjunction used to make comparisons between two things. It's used when you're saying one thing is better, worse, more, or less than another thing.
   - **Example:** "She is taller than her brother." (Comparing heights.)
   - **Example:** "I would rather stay home than go to the party." (Expressing preference or choice.)

Remembering the difference:

- "Then" is used for time, sequence, or consequence.
- "Than" is used for making comparisons.

Effect vs Affect

"Effect" is a noun and "affect" can be used as a noun or a verb, though it's *usually* used as a verb. See examples below.

1. **Effect (noun):** "Effect" refers to the result or consequence of an action or event. It indicates what happens as a result of something else.
   - **Example:** "The medicine had a positive effect on her health." (The positive change in her health was the result of taking the medicine.)
   - **Example:** "The new law had unintended effects on the economy." (The changes in the economy were the consequences of the new law.)

2. **Affect (verb):** "Affect" is *usually* used as a verb, meaning to influence or produce a change in something.

   - **Example:** "The loud noise affected her concentration." (In this sentence, "affect" is used to indicate that the loud noise influenced or disturbed her ability to concentrate.)
   - **Example:** "The medication may affect certain individuals differently."(Here, "affect" is used to suggest that the medication may produce different reactions or effects in different people.)

3. **Affect (noun):** "Affect" is less commonly used as a noun but refers to the outward display of someone's emotions, mood, or demeanor.
   - **Example:** "Her affect was cheerful despite the difficult circumstances." (Her outward display of mood or emotion was cheerful.)
   - **Example:** "His flat affect concerned the doctors." (His lack of outward emotion or expression concerned the doctors.)

Lets vs Let's

"Let's" and "lets" are both related to the verb "let," but they are used differently:

1. **Let's:** "Let's" is a contraction of "let us." It's used to suggest or propose that someone, including the speaker, should do something together. It's a combination of the verb "let" and the pronoun "us."
   - **Example:** "Let's go to the movies." (Let us go to the movies.)
   - **Example:** "Let's have dinner together." (Let us have dinner together.)

2. **Lets:** "Lets" is the third-person singular form of the verb "let." It's used when someone or something allows or permits something else to happen.
   - **Example:** "He lets his dog run freely in the park." (He allows his dog to run freely.)
   - **Example:** "The teacher lets her students ask questions." (The teacher permits her students to ask questions.)

Remembering the difference:
- "Let's" is a contraction of "let us" and is used to make suggestions or proposals involving the speaker and others.

"Lets" is the third-person singular form of the verb "let" and is used to indicate permission or allowance.

Made in the USA
Las Vegas, NV
19 September 2024

95528607R00057